All the Days After

SPEAK FIRE PUBLISHING

JF Nickerson

W̲RITER'S N̲OTES

Growing up, when I visited with my Auntie and Godmother Helen Gibson, I would say, "I love you, always and forever." Her reply would be, "I love you , always and forever and all the days after."

Finding out later in life this was our special saying to each other.

Now, I am sharing it with the world.

JF Nickerson

CONTENTS

All the Days After

1

LOVE

Love is?
Love gives...
Love accepts...
Does Love have
conditions?

What is Love?

Love, Love, Love...
Is Love overrated?
Love judge?
What does Love?

Love... You can't stop.
Love...
Love is ME.
LOVE.

Always and Forever and All the Days After

Dedicated to Helen Gibson

I was
taught how
to love
without
conditions
Love taught
me when I
was a little

girl
Love taught
me about
my beauty

Love taught
me pure
innocence
Love taught
me I am
okay
I was
taught how
to Love the
beauty of
the color of
my skin
The beauty
of my hair
The beauty
of my space
in between
my teeth

Love
taught so
many things
Love taught
without
judging
Love taught
without

Love
without
shame
Love, LOVE,
Always and
Forever and
All The
Days After...
LOVE

I LOVE YOU BECAUSE

I Love you because?

There is greatness within you,

>   And while you might not believe in yourself

I believe in you and your greatness.

I Love you because?

>   The most amazing Love of all is...

I Love you because?

>   You are you...

>   Not because of anything...

I Love you because?

>   You are who you are.

I love you always and forever, and ALL
the days after,

Not some of the days,
but ALL of the days after.

4

LOVE DOES

Love Protects...

Love Respects....

Love Prepares for all things...

I LOVE YOU!!!! ALWAYS and forever...

AND ALL THE DAYS AFTER.

Stop,

               Stop,

                              Stop,

        ALL THE DAYS AFTER.

There is, no?

Stop, there is...

        No end for Love.

TRUE LOVE

True Love, The Creator

Of Love...

Love...

Love prepared a place...

Not just for a day or year

but for...

Love...

It came with food, water, air...

Love...

The Ultimate, Playpen, Playground...

Everything and

Anything we would need.

So, if LOVE?

Provided for us then, what does *after* look like?

Love you,

always and forever,

and all the days after.

WHAT DOES LOVE

What does Love look like

Would you Love me if...

What is your if? What is my if?

Should I even care what your if is?

If you Love me, what does Love look like?

When will I truly understand your Love, how you Love, why you Love, when you Love?

Is your Love contingent upon me doing this, or me doing that?

What does your Love look like?

If I fail,

will you still love me?

IF I DON'T MEET YOUR EXPECTATIONS

If I don't meet your expectations, would you still love me?

What does your love look like.

Is your love always and forever, and All the Days After?

Can you comprehend

"that" type of love?

8

<u>L</u>OVE YOU

Love You because

I am you. You are me.

I Love You Because

I could not.

Could not what?

Stop,

Love for you or towards you.

Stop towards or for you.

Love

No.

I Love you because, Love has no end.

Only the begin and all the days after

Love you

THEIR LOVE, OUR LOVE

Our Love is.

Our Love is always.

Their Love is, uncontrollable.

By others.

Uncontrollable.

What.

Yes, unstoppable.

Their love, our love continues pressing.

Pressing, Moving.

Moving Pressing.

Unstoppable.

Our Love continues.   Their What?   Love

When all is said and done.   Done and spoke.

Their Love, Our Love

10

<u>THEY TRIED</u>

They Tried it.

They Tried, what.

To end our Love

Why?

Not good enough

Why? Broken

Who, what?

Why, what?

They tried to end our Love.

Tried? Love

Love. Tried

Love? Wins

Tried? Love

Love won.

What? Love

Wins

      Unconditional love won.

11

<u>BECAUSE OF YOU</u>

Because of You, I...

I Live.

I Love.

I have breath.

Because of You, I am.

Because of You, I do this, I do that.

Because of You, I can do

Because of You, I am great.

I am what?

You heard,

Great.

Because of You,

I'm able to love.

Say it.

Because of You.

          Because of You I am you.

Because of You, I am Me.

                      Because of You.

12

<u>I AM</u>

I AM the person you wanted to define.

I AM the person you wanted to kill.

I AM not.

I AM great.   I AM, who?   I AM not.

I AM wonderfully created.I was created to do wonderful things.

I AM wonderfully created.

I AM a creator,

I AM Me

I AM self-determined.

I AM not.

I AM not

I Am not stoppable.

Did you catch that?

I AM walking into...

Into all things I desire.

I AM unstoppable

I AM capable

Do you hear.?

Do you hear, Me

I AM who...

I define.

Myself to be.

Who am I?

Mr. White to you.

13

<u>MULTIPLE STREAMS</u>

Streams

Multiple Streams.

    Streams

Whatever, whoever desires

     Multiple streams

    Streams

Streams.   Yes, *streams*.

  I live by.   I walk, by.   I work by.

Multiple streams, while you sleep.

Why streams?

Think streams.

    Streams

        Streams

Multiple streams

Steams work

While you sleep

Trust the process

Believe in the process

If you know, then you know

Multiple streams

BLANK PAGES

Why Blank?

Blank pages.

Do I dream?

Why dream?

Blank pages

Put down

Create it

Make it

Write it

Color it

Blank

Pages

Beautiful works of art

Canvas full of what?

Blank,

Blank.

Blank pages

Dream on

Create on.

What?

I create

I change

We change

Put it down.

This change

To beauty

I changed, this amazing once

Blank page

Into,

Into,

Into what?

Into Color,

Into Dreams,

Blank pages, what?

Into letters

Letters into words,

Into thoughts

Blank pages.

Into whatever I can imagine.

I can dare to change

You can dare to change

Change anything, everything.

Into a beautiful masterpiece

Stop,

Wait,

Look,

Investigate.

Investigate, the blank pages.

Blank pages are no longer

Blank pages

A work of art.

No longer

Blank pages

LOVE IS ALL THINGS

Love sees things

All things.

Love can

Change a thing

Love is not afraid

Love is

I am hurt.

I am wounded

I am what.

Love is all things

Love is

Love changes the narrative

Love changes

Love is pure

Love is Joy

Love is more than

What you can ever imagine.

Love is.

No limits,

Find Love,

Love finds all things

Live to Love

Love to be pure in all things

Love is

Love Is all things

16

<u>NOTHING</u>

Nothing

My mind has nothing.

This is the why.

The why is

I am here, nothing.

Nothing, nothing turns into

What, frustration

Nothing is an attack

To the mind.

Turn nothing

into something

Something

I have something

My mind is always creating

Something

Something is not nothing.

17

TIME OUT

How do you move?

Time out

Time in

No

Know

No time out

Why do you move

You move why

Move

Move

Time out

Plan the next move

Time out

Love the move

Time out

—JF Nickerson

GRANDMA'S WINE MADE WITH LOVE

DEDICATED TO UNCLE DANNY/GOD DAD

Wine made with love

Black raspberry

Grandma's wine

Brother and I would try

Grandma's wine

Grandma's wine, black raspberry

Made with love

Brother and I would try

Hogtie

Hogtie

What?

Grandma's wine of black raspberry

Jugs and jugs of black raspberry

Grandma's wine

Jugs of black raspberry wine

Took two to pour

Grandma's wine

Black raspberry—Grandma

Wine before her time

Grandma's wine

I wish I could have tried

Tried black raspberry

Black raspberry wine made with love

That's Grandma's wine

Grandma was before her time

Black raspberry

Wine

You thought you wouldn't get caught

Touching Grandma's wine

Bet' not get caught touching

Hogtie hogtied!

Don't get caught taking

Grandma's wine

Black raspberry

Black Raspberry

Made with love

Nothing like

I heard there was nothing like

Grandma's wine

Grandma's wine

That was Grandma's wine

That is Grandma's wine

Made with love

Black raspberry wine

COMFORT WITHIN

Comfort within what

Comfort within growth

Comfort within change

No, stop

Hold up

Why

Comfort within what

Comfort

Comfort within all things

Says, who

Comfort within, NO

Comfort within

When I say, not you say

Comfort within

Yes,

Comfort within

20

WAIT TO DIE

Continue to live

Wait to die

You wait for them to die

Why

How long will you wait for them to die

Continue to live

Live as long as you want to live

Why do you wait

Or

Expect them to...

Age

Health wait to

Wait to

Live

Or

Die

Live

Continue to Live

21

<u>INTERMISSION</u>

Love,

this is

from my thoughts.

Not to say, that this *is to say,*

This is how love should be, or interpreted,

or the meaning of it.

We all have our own thoughts and feelings on the meaning of

Love

and how to accept it or reject it.

22

JUST KNOW

Just Know

What

Who defines you

Just know

Just know you define you

Just know that

What that

Defines

What

Defines greatness,

Defines power,

Defines peace

Peace defines

Soundness defines

Greatness defines

Just know

You define

Just know

Passion defines

Just know

23

ANOTHER YEAR

Another year

Is here

As another year is here

Of you not being here

As I realize

I want to do

I can't do

As I realize the pain

Is still here

As I

As I realize,

Don't temp me

Another year

SAYING GOODBYE 57

So here we are

Where are we

Here we are

Saying goodbye 57

57

OLD 57

Have you been good

Old 57

you called it quits to some

57 saying goodbye

57 your time is almost over

57 you're moving over

57

57

Oh 57

It's almost time

In other places

of the world

58 would be here

58 are you ready

58 what do you have to say

58 brings great things

Saying goodbye 57 and welcome 58

Make great thing happen

57/58

364

MY NAME

What's in a Name

Many things are in a Name

What is in My Name

JF Nickerson

Love is in my name

Respect is in my name

Power is in my name

Desire is in my name

My Name

Your Name

Name is everything

My Name

JF Nickerson

There is power

There is greatness

There is authority

There is creativity

In my name

I define my name

Love created my name

My Name

There is Greatness

There is Power

There is Authority

There is Creativity

Just know my name

Is not

What you call me

My Name

Is mine

Not yours to change

It's *my name*

JF Nickerson

26

PREPARATION

Time has come

It's time for

What, why

Preparation

Preparation yes

Yes preparation

Preparation for great promises

Prep for arrival

Preparation for anything

Prep for everything

Battle

Prep for battle.

Preparation to move forward

Preparation is how I move

Preparation is how I win the battles

It's time or

Past time

Time is preparation

IF LOVE COULD WAIT

If Love could

Wait

What would wait look like

Why

Would

Love

Wait?

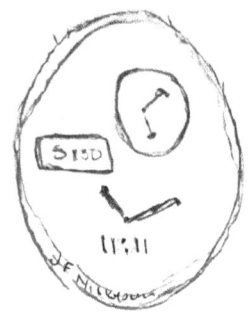

How long would

Love, wait

If love could wait

Would it change

Would it do

Do what

        Love is waiting for

           You.

           Me.

           Us.

           Them.

If Love could wait

WOULD LOVE WAIT

Stop prolonging it

Prolonging what?

Love

If love could wait

Would it wait

If love could wait

What would it wait for

Stop prolonging for love

Prolonging Love

Stop

Who would it wait for

Love is *here*

TOWARDS YOU

Moving towards you

Towards you

Preparation

Towards you

Don't run

Receive

Towards dreams

Aspirations

Desires

Towards you

Greatness, great things

Everything positive

Towards you

Creativity, towards you

You're moving towards

Power

Love

Protection towards you

Love towards you

Towards *you*

30

ONE LOVE

Our Love

One Love

To be continued

No

Stop

One Love

Our Love

Our Love, One Love

Who Love

Our Love

One Love

31

STAGE SET

The Stage has been set

Stage set

For

You

Me

What

ACT 1

Expression

Expression of love

What

After love

Toward love

To be loved

Expression of love

Stage Set

Love

Please take your mark

Stage Set

32

FEAR, SCARED

Is it Fear

or am I Scared

Shaking uncontrollable

No, stop

Overcome with

What comes next

Change the script

What change

Mind racing

Racing

Why

The unknown or known

Why

Change the storyline

Is it really

Wait, stop

No, stop

Can't shake this thing

Run

Drive

Get out the way

Fear, scared

Of

Why, what

Make it stop

Stop, what

Change the

Change

Stop shaking

Body reaction

Mind racing

Eyes

Can't what

Believe what

I'm seeing

Fear,

Scared,

PTSD

All real

What

Yes, right now,

Emotion overload

Run from

Drive from

What, wait

Change

Not expected

Stop

What is it

What was it

F=False

E=Evidence

A=Appearing

R=Real

This not real

Or

Is it

Rain uncontrollable

Water everywhere

Get off the road

Fear,

Scared

Tornado

So, I thought

Change the script

33

THANK YOU

How often can you say people

Tell you

Thank you

Thank You

For your

Time

Energy

Thoughts

Services

Love

Thank you

For

Being you

Who you are

The good

The bad

The ugly

Why

Because

I see you

Or

You see

You, hear

Thank your

Thank you

For

Love

Loving

Accepting without conditions

Or

Contingent upon

Thank you

Love thanks you

34

ALL I KNOW

All I know

I can't live without

You.

I can't breathe without

You.

Love, I miss you

               All I know

                               All I know

I hear you

Your calls

Your laughter

Your voice

All I know

How did I get here

All I know

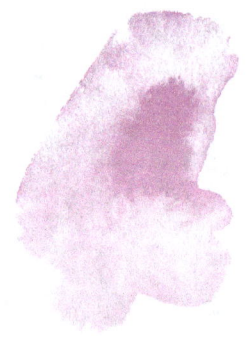

35

<u>LISTEN</u>

Why

Listen

To you

How come

Listen to whom

Why do you

What?

Act like

You wanted my attention

Why not?

You do

I do

Listen

Do you HEAR me

HELLO

Do you ever listen

Why do you

What

Answer that way

Do you hear me

Listen

Stop and listen

You don't listen

I don't answer

The way

You like

I heard you

Every word you said

I can repeat it, if you like

Listen

36

THE CRAP

Crap or trash

Good or bad

Ugly or pretty

Crap

Say what

The crap

The crap is all in what

The interpretation

Or

In the

In the what

Eyes of the

Mind of the

Thoughts of the

Creator

Or

Beholder

Behold

The crap

Wonderfully made

Beautiful

Amazing

Authentic

The crap

Created out of

Going through

Joy

Pain

Life

The crap

Is real

An expression of

What is with

The crap

Keep pushing

P=pray

U=until

S=something

H=happens

The crap

Is not

What

Or

Is

Whatever

You

Determine

It too

Too what

Be

Change the narrative

Which are

What are

You

Creator

Beholder

Or

Both

The crap

37

LOVE MADE A WAY

Love

Made a way

To

Walk away

Leave comfort of my father's home

Love

Made a way

Protect

Family

Love made

conversation

Conversation made

Love

Love made

understanding

Love made

What

A way to

Listen

Love

Made a way

38

DREAMS

Dreams

Became

Blueprints

Dreams

Became

Aspirations

Dreams

Became

Visions

Dreams

Become

More

Blueprints are created

Blueprints by creators

Dreams More dreams

Dreams

39

<u>MOVE</u>

Move

What — Why

Move — Movement

Grow, move

Why

Just move

Move

Movement

Movement brings health

Move

Love to Move

Move

40

<u>LOVE YOU LIKE THIS</u>

Who

Loves you *like this*

Why

Love is like

What

Different meaning

Different interpretations

Different non-limitations

Don't judge

No judgment of what someone's

Love you *like this*

Relationship

Love you *like this*

Why

Because I can

Love you *like this*

Love like this

Pure

Kind

Support, protect

Love like this

Freedom

Love you like this

Created all things

Love you *like this*

41

<u>REST, PEACE</u>

Peace

Rest

Love, peace

Oneness

Wholeness

Rest

You don't

What

You don't understand

Not meant for you

Understand

Rest, peace

Peace, my peace

Rest, my rest

Rest in Grandma's peace

Grandma's peace

Grandma's rest

Grandma's love

Rest, peace

42

∞

<u>57</u> TO YOU

Growth happened *57*

Change happened *57*

Challenges happened *57*

57 What

Pain in *57*

Looking in *57*

Change *57*

Not

What

You think

57 to You

43

WATCHING WHAT

Watching growth

Watching love

What

Watching change

Watching

Love watches

Watching you sleep

Watching you play

Watching you grow

Watching you learn

Watching all things

Watching what

Watching love

Love watches

Without

Rose colored glasses

Love watches

Love

44

SPECIAL THANKS

I would like to thank everyone who took the time out their busy day to read over and provide their prospective of my writing.

Just know it means more than you would ever realize.

Vera, Traci, Teri, Carol, Carlon, Ivory, Angie, JoJo, Debbie and Tiffany—my circle. And my other circle people you know who are, I thank you.

I love you, always and forever and ALL the days after!!

–JF Nickerson